The Last of the Bee Lovely Murmur Days

For Colleen –
Love from your friend,
Debbie!
Christmas – 2014

The Last of the Bee Lovely Murmur Days

Poetry & Art
by
Debbie Bumstead

Printed in the United States of America
ISBN-13:**978-1503250680**
ISBN-10:1503250687

In Memory of Phillip William Winans

Contents

Dapple Checker Leaf

Rain-Cleaned Hearts

The World Goes Along So Beautifully

Rules

(written in 1974 and so far scrupulously followed for 40 years)

Dapple Checker Leaf

A Snowflake Falls

A snowflake falls from the sky;
Another falls with another sigh;
Many will fall, many will fly,
When the clouds pass over, by and by.

Snow Forests

Along highways through forests of snow,
In passing we see how the pine limb bundles
Are melted by the sun and crashing go,
In clumps and shattered bits, by flights and tumbles,
While the branches freed, shake like a wet dog
And the snow falls in drifts on the ground.
A crime witnessed, pictures we take, events we log,
Of the act itself and how the body of snow was found;
But it is happening up and down mountains, far away,
In places we can't take our eyes to witness;
In all those secret reaches, we'll never see the way
Snow from trees falls there, secretly,
   And in snow forests,
     will secretly rest.

A Visit to the Fish Hatchery

We drove the curves, turned in at a gate, and
Crackled gravel down to the buildings by the river.
We wandered on foot past the outdoor tanks;
Above one a young fish caught on the aerator panel
Flipped uselessly, gaped its gills; unable to help,
We watched and urged with our hearts for a stronger flip,
Or wished with our own hands that fish had hands.
Indoors the smaller tanks held black swarms of things
That swirled away from the looming shapes of us.
Later we walked down to the river,
The roiling, foaming, freezing river,
Goal of all the hatchery fishes; we stood
Above on the bank, caught ourselves in the unwatered air,
But unlike the trapped fish, content there.

Spring Hurts

Spring hurts
By its knobs of green
Pushing to be out. Why can't I
Be new each year? It hurts to watch
Sprouts of rose leaves and spears from bulbs
In new green thrusting -- I'm skin and meat;
Nothing new grows out; Flowers don't bloom
From the top of me. It hurts to feel
Plant crisp, plant fresh, spring grass
Under my feet of flesh.

In Spring

Like unfurled wings against the sky,
Spring in my body, lift.
From my hands, birds, fly,
Beat out dreams along the wind drift.

Like an image reborn to die,
Spring in its meaning, nest.
From my hands, birds, fly,
Dream out life and then travel home to rest.

Magic Mornings

Spring mornings break early,
In the empty city streets;
A friend and I are out by chance,
While others are still asleep.

Humans have lost their city,
Having deserted it for their homes;
Now the dawn-enchanted animals
Inherit the streets, to strut and roam.

Inherit the empty streets and wander,
An orange cat under a parked car,
Pigeons down the center of avenues,
A crow picking pennies stuck in the tar.

While the city is soft-gray and silent,
An ugly dog with an ear nick,
Seems to bark into the dawn-coming air,
    "Magic! Magic! Magic!"

We wish we were those animals,
And owned the lonely hours;
Then we, too, would wander and call,
For Spring dawns and magic powers.

Spring Summer Whisper

Panda swamp sprouts and a
Wee dew giraffe; look at -- my
Strawberry shy dream of
Sun earth and
Awakening to find myself turned to
Dusty tickle beetles
That have all wandered away.

Squash maroon child and
Dapple checker leaf --
When I've lost my eyeglasses the
Moon blade forest is waterpainted on
Turquoise tremble sneeze silk
That someone up above is rippling.

Cockatoo forest curl,
Ribbon blush hair --
I have run with the
Flower dappling sapling sun;
Giggle float shiver blooms --
It's been a bee-lovely murmur day
In my watermelon world.

Loosaapa, My Horse

Loosaapa is my mother
She carries me on her back
Stars rise up from her spots
Butterflies come out her ears
Loosaapa, my horse mother
She runs so fast
Birds fly out of her hooves

Loosaapa is my mother
She carries me on her back
Her tears are purple dragonflies
Her teeth are champing moons
Loosaapa, my horse mother
She runs so fast
Birds fly out of her hooves

Flowers

In late Fall there are no flowers;
The myrtle blossoms are gone, the roses dead;
Decayed petals under pruned stem towers
Are, without dignity, fed
To the garden earth with ashes thrown
From fireplace piles, with wet fallen leaves,
And apple peels, and bananas turned brown,
And horse manure -- the spent flowers grieve.
They once were bright and stiff with pride;
Camellias, roses, jasmine, elegantly dressed,
Expensively scented; and when one died,
Another took its place, identically fashioned.
They once were so highly admired,
They were cut and put in the house,
On the mantel, on the table, in the fired
Ceramic bowl, in the beautiful Chinese vase
Worth hundreds of dollars!
But now Winter comes, all the flowers are dead;
They return to the earth with egg shells and collards,
And must learn to accept the crude dignity
                Of the compost bed.

peace
9-11-01

Burning Leaves

Fire is Autumn's bosom
On which we throw the leaves,
All golden pixies, light and lissome,
Dancing around the bloodied trees.
The air is sharp and lively,
And the pixies, full of fun,
Settle to the fire, reluctantly;
Then quickly comes the dying sun,
And the leaves of golden pixies
      Flicker in the night
          and are gone.

Still, Rabbit, Still

A dog barks far away;
The wind creaks in the windmill;
Every sound has something to say
To busy ears that are rarely still.

A garden carrot in early May;
A flowery field on a grassy hill;
Every smell has something to say
To a twitching nose that is rarely still.

Fuzzy cottontails hop at play;
Racing birds swoop with a trill;
Every movement has something to say
To thumping feet that are rarely still.

But when the coyote hunts at break of day;
And the owl passes searching for a kill;
Then the rabbits, quiet, in the thickets stay
Hidden ears, nose, and legs now still, still, still

Trowbridge Hill

Grandpa in your adobe house with Grandbee,
Surrounded by hills, boulders, and yellow weeds,
You polished stone, outdoors, planted seeds,
And spoke, we always say, very rarely.
Through your rocky canyons the family--
We children--used to hike, until our needs
Brought us back to Grandbee's picnic feeds;
Your were there, too, sitting somewhere pensively.
You and I, Grandpa, were two quiet ones;
Our eyes met secretly, with stolen glances sent
Across the heads of relatives--oh, this path runs
Up into the wild brush; under tree limbs bent
Your ashes buried here feel all the seasons' suns,
And like the enduring rocks around me, you are still,
                                                    Still silent.

Rain-Cleaned Heart

The Sea Stone

This rock fits against the hand.
It is the bone of a lost Indian, a pebble in a necklace,
    an arrow wrapped twice with thread.
The white stone lines running through the gray are welts
    drawn-with the claws of a prehistoric tiger,
    they are the crushed teeth of sharks,
    the stretched strands of an otter's intestine.
This rock fits closely, dark like the fur of an island seal,
    cool with the turnings of years in a northern sea.
It is a seagull for soaring, for skipping, for flying in the air.
It is a pelican diving miles from shore, a fish rippling oceans.
It is a dark-skinned man plunging into mystery,
    the crossing white threads mermaid arms
    wrapped around his chest.
When he comes to shore he stands, rolled and turned
    clean by the waves, glistens,
    wet like a sea stone.

Watermelon Song

I love having you burst me
Open watermelon
All my luscious
All my water
All open dripping
Watermelon
I love having you burst me
Open watermelon
All my red
All my sugar
All dripping sweet seeds
Love me! Love me!
Love me all open!

Washington Rain

The steady rain of Washington state,
In summer, on vacation, helps one forget--
Or not forget, but resign the fate
Of love never woken, of love never let.
The rain falls like washing that wound;
Pressure is applied, pain is forgotten,
And the trees spread against the cloud
Like broken blood flows into cotton.
Then the forest opens its rain-cleaned heart
And seems with bright happiness flushed;
It grows as if there is beauty in the hurt
After the wound is washed.

A Leaden Mark

A leaden mark appeared on the page;
I know like a knife it gleamed at you,
And twisted, not a scratch or a graze,
But straight to the vitals; red and blue,
The blood I brought forth with a word,
Coated your last days with struggle and pain--
You died; though the pen marks are now blurred,
Keep the letter in afterlife; the lesson is plain--
               Do not love again.

A Cat's Love

My little cat cuddles up to me, warm upon my lap;
His purr, his gentle eyes, the comfort of all that,
Releases the burning tears, unscrews the broken tap
Of lost human love; so inferior to that of a cat,
Yet how I search for that fault in man,
And finding it, only to curse it and cry,
And end up as before, stretched out on the divan,
Loveless, hopeless, disgusted with that human lie,
While my cat, so perfect a friend, tenderly winks; at least
               I am loved by him.

California Oranges

Debbie BW

No Matter How Deep

No matter how deep
Into what pond you have dropped it,
Into what deserted pit,
Covered and hid with rocks;
Still like a watch ticking it mocks;
No matter how deep
With what earth you have flung it,
With what anger stamped till it split,
Though the knots and bulges bled;
It throbs, alive, alive, not dead.
No matter how deep
Even in cities, under houses,
Enmeshed in concrete instead of blouses,
Out from shirts and far down below streets;
No matter how deep you have buried your heart---
                                   It still beats.

7

The World Goes Along So Beautifully

Portrait of My Green and Golden Year

We're all very small in our beautiful world
Of reaching green shapes and shadows;
The yellow shines down canyons of trees,
And the brook curls over sand to the sea.

Our family's brave and new, like pioneers;
Mom's a splash of love, Dad is magic blue;
Big brothers explorer tan, and me peachy pink,
Little girl in rainy wilderness, soaking up new life.

The picture of our year in Washington state
Glows golden – Look how clean, how bright
Our lives became when we left the desert
And discovered a forest, an ocean of our own.

Long ago I rode my stick horse on fairy paths,
Spoke to spirits of trees, and fell deep deep
Into a wonder-filled beauty that's never left me,
Not once, in all the dusty years that followed.

Child of Divorce

We're like buildings standing in a line
But never touching, and the streets
Don't lead anywhere near, but always away,

And the wind swirls around us and
Whistles in the empty areas between us.
If only one of us could open a door;

Bridges need to be built, busy skyways
To connect each of us to the other,
But it's not going to happen, not today.

Or tomorrow, or for years. I've lost
The ability to grow, like a building
Under construction, suddenly abandoned.

The sun still shines, the birds still fly,
But there's a gap between how I began
And now, where I should be, but can't reach.

Wall of Shyness

I like my safe and secret garden
Behind the red brick wall;
Here I have my little life
Of things to do and ways to be,
And nothing here frightens me.

Chinks in my wall let in light
From the outside world;
Here I stand sometimes to look;
Still hidden and safe, I often see
How the world goes along so beautifully.

Then someone opened my garden door;
Someone beckoned; I took a step;
A ray of sunshine lit my face;
Another step, and I saw the key --
Only by going through will I be free.

Together We Travel

A road curves, rushing through the past –
Our little car like a jolt of memory
Zips up and down, around and around --
Oh, the trips we took, the journeys we planned,
The paths we followed, the years we traveled.
Forests of flickering light and shadow,
How many forests we sped through
Like a swooping bird, and every time,
Every time, glances, smiles, loving together
The limitless beauty of the trees.
Oh, all the stops at mini-marts and cafes,
All the food we ate, all the restrooms we visited!
All the people we saw, speaking to some,
Watching others without a word,
Everywhere we went, children playing
Women talking, men laughing,
Every single one an individual
With a whole life's trip bundled up inside
Like a treasure map -- they are all out there now
Somewhere in the world we once traveled.

Remember the motels, the cool clean rooms
Folding around us the quiet of rest,
And all the times we made love in strange beds,
Far away from home, each encounter
Like some exciting best-loved and well-known
Journey within a journey. Then --
Mornings, extra bright with sometimes sun
Sometimes snow, and you'd say,
"The weather is a character,"

And we'd drive onward, explorers
Discovering our own bit of earth,
While within, on the map of memories,
We marked each turn, each curve,
Each mountain, each valley,
Each red-pinned point of interest.
Remember? We smoothed out all the map's
Rumpled creases using our loving hearts;
With our hands clasped and a light kiss,
We shared smiles for the infinite journey.

The Landscape of Disease

I'm sorry, so sorry, the dangerous landscape
Of this strange planet
Has caught you in its sticky air --
Watch out!
Creatures of microscopic horror,
Tentacles sweeping, reach for you --
Stay on your path, keep going,
Don't stop!
Whatever you do, don't stop --
Oh, don't stop, dear.
Their gelatinous bodies prickled
With cursed genes pump like octopi
Low over the slime, threatening you --
Look up!
Not at the black sunbirth of another
Evil disease, no!
Look up at the shining sky, see beyond
The boundaries of this clinging scape.
Look up and search.
You might discern birds flying, singing --
You might hear a lovely song
As you travel your path, my dear,
You might hear a lovely song.

Grief

Mountains like waves on a giant sea --
Hiding the path of my way from me.
Where is beyond sorrow? I'm left behind.
Golden meadow, lost island of mine,
Obscured by tears, a thousand miles away --
By long journey, I'll reach its peace some day.

Loneliness

I've ridden waves of darkness long in the night,
My brightness dimmed by colors without light.
Sunshine beckons on the horizon, far away from me,
As, separated from the shore, I sail this lonely sea.

The Spiral Path

A spiral path leads me
Along my daily descent,
Each upturn a curl of hope
Or a stray lightening of spirit,
But each downturn a sinking
One step further of the heart's troubles.
Reverberations of memory and desire
Overshadow like encircling trees
The pathway of my sadness,
Whipping their branches at me,
Every sting a pain I can hardly bear.
And then -- I leap from spiral's end
Into the darkness of release
To find the soothing pool of tears
That saves me from falling too far.

Rules
(First written in 1974 & so far scrupulously followed for the last 40 years)

Rules

Rule: You must never think you are special or think that someone else thinks you are special. You may have an inkling, a hope, but you mustn't be sure, ever.

Rule: Every day, besides your evening exercises, you must do one very active thing -- play tennis against the backboard, run from a class to your car, run around the living room 20 times with the dog, etc.

Rule: You my not ever say anything against anyone else, you are not to say what you think of someone if it is bad. You may say aloud how someone makes you feel, but you must always make that distinction--that this is a feeling and not a statement of fact.

Rule: You must never be too lazy to get up from sitting or lying down to do something -- close the window, get a snack for you and your friend, answer the door, etc.

Rule: You are required to treat every person with the same care and kindness as you treat the people you love (though, of course, it will not be with the same intensity of feeling or the same knowledge --knowing the people whom you love know you love them).

Rule: You are not ever allowed to tell or live an untruth. You may pretend and imagine and tell stories but the principle of truth must always be clear and shining in your life.

Rules for Punching, Pushing, Wrestling, etc.

If somebody hits you, you may hit them back. If you hit somebody, they may hit you back. But if they hit back harder than you hit them, you may hit them again, hard enough to make up for their harder hit. But if you hit harder than enough to make up for it they may hit back again.

These are the reasons you may validly use to punch a person. They tease you or tickle you. They push or pull or call you a name. You may hit a person for these reasons and they cannot hit you back unless you hit too hard.

Always hit in the upper arm. You may, if you think wise, stick one finger's knuckle up for a sharper pain.

You may punch for love.

Rules for Running and Walking, Skipping, etc.

When you are out walking, if you come to a hill you must run up it.

If a place you are going to is within walking distance, you must not drive.

When you are happy and singing inside, run, run.

If the sun is warm on your back, walk slowly, wander.

With some friends you may skip.

If you have been cooped up too long in a classroom, when it lets out, run as fast as you can.

If you are going by the way of which there is a curb, you are required to walk and balance on that curb.

Rules for Magic

Magic at its best is spontaneous. Here are some general rules.

If you find a magic object, put it in a magic place.

If you hear a meadowlark's song in the morning; expect a magic day.

The songs and calls of birds will enchant you; listen.

A magic tree is strong; touch its leaves often.

A magic place -- a walnut tree grove, a glade beside a pond, a rocky ravine -- has even more strength, go there as often as you can.

Your name is magic--when somebody uses it they are touching you magically; listen to the way they touch you.

Rule; Always do what you say you will do and if you can't, say you can't. You must keep your word; remember, you must try to do that which you intend to do. If you say you're going to be somewhere at a certain time, be there. If you say you are going to give someone something, give it.
Rule: You have no right to bore people. If you think you are being boring, leave. Stop whatever is boring or learn to do it in a more fascinating way.
Rule: If you make a rule, obey it.

Things You Have Permission To Do
 If you don't like being where you are, or with the people you're with, you may run away.

If you are too bashful to answer a question, you may say, "I don't know."
It's all right to be shy -- smile at the floor, fiddle with your watch, doodle, etc.
You don't have to talk if you can't.
You may be a brat as long as it doesn't hurt anyone.
You may cry.

Rule: You must love, you must be honest, you must see beauty and be good and kind.
Rule: Love.

Rule: Love

About the Author

Debbie Bumstead has self-published four books previously, and if only you would read them, you would see how full of vibrant troubled joyous life they are! *Apricot* and *The Dream Time* are memoirs of growing-up days in small town America during the 50s and 60s with a quirky artistic family, fabulous friends, and brilliant teachers. *Dear Dr. Pullias* continues the story of a young woman's life by epistolary means: ten years of correspondence between Debbie and her famous friend, Earl V. Pullias, Ph.D. *The Destruction of Alice*, a novel, is an attempt to express the difficulty of a girl once raped seeking her first experience of true love.

Debbie is also prolific in artwork. She is the illustrator of the Smileytooth series of dental hygiene books by Dr. Gary Nelson. She has sold many of her pet paintings and accepts commissions. Please contact her at: happydogart@gmail.com or visit her websites: DebbieBumsteadianLit.com; RenoRoundAbout.blogspot.com;

BumsteadianArt.blogspot.com; and
EarlVPulliasPhD.blogspot.com

Made in the USA
San Bernardino, CA
21 November 2014